KU-175-905

The Resurrection– Fact or Fiction?

RICHARD BEWES

A LION BOOK

Published by
Lion Publishing plc
Sandy Lane West, Oxford, England
ISBN 0 7459 1549 3
Lion Publishing
850 North Grove Avenue, Elgin, Illinois 60120, USA
ISBN 0 7459 1549 3
Albatross Books Pty Ltd
PO Box 320, Sutherland, NSW 2232, Australia
ISBN 0 7324 0017 1

First Edition 1989
10 9 8 7 6 5 4

Acknowledgments
Photographs by Lion Publishing: David Alexander, page 9, David
Townsend, pages 17, 21, 25, 37 and 41; ZEFA UK, pages 5, 12, 29, 32,
44–45; and reproduced by courtesy of John Rylands University
Library, Manchester, page 14

Printed and bound in Slovenia

CONTENTS

Just supposing   4

The greatest question   7

And now for the rest of the news . . . 11

A confusing day   14

Running feet   16

I refuse to answer   19

A question of evidence   22

The psychological barrier   27

The moral barrier   31

The doubter   34

The resurrection body   39

A way of life   43

Check the facts!   48

JUST SUPPOSING

'I feel sorry for you Christians,' said the taxi driver over his shoulder.

He looked anything but sorry. His shoulders were shaking with laughter.

'There you all are,' he went on, 'pinning everything on your belief in an after-life; working, praying, giving up everything. And then when you get to the end you'll discover there's nothing there after all!' Once more he was convulsed with laughter.

I laughed too. It seemed the right response. But then I began to try and turn the tables on my materialistic critic.

'It's all very well,' I said, 'but even supposing you were right and I was wrong; that there's no heaven, no judgment, no after-life or anything like that. Even so, I still come out with the advantage over you! Here I am—deluded, according to you—making my way through life, firm in my conviction that life isn't the product of chance. Convinced with millions of others—in my delusion—that we're here on this world for a purpose, that a man called Jesus Christ has beaten back death on behalf of us all. Fired and motivated—in my delusion—by the sense of his living presence with me every day. I then come to the end of my days on earth, believing that my energies have all been spent for a lasting purpose; I go out into eternity and then in fact—if you are right—I won't

The Christian faith is not limited to people of any race or background. Anyone can begin a new life with God's help.

even have the disappointment of knowing that I was deluded!'

'But you,' I continued; 'supposing you are wrong and I am right? There you are, struggling to make a living and to earn enough money to keep yourself together—and you don't even know why! Trying to make sense of existence; living life off your own batteries, hoping for the best, fighting off illness and decay for as long as possible, finally losing your powers and then having to accept that you must die.'

'And then at the end you are in for the most terrible shock. You will find yourself confronted by the very

5

person you'd ignored all your life. You will have to realize that everything you've been living for was wasted. It has all been for nothing. Just supposing such a thing could be enough to bring you to a halt and make you do a U-turn!'

In fact, when it comes to the Christian claim of the resurrection of Jesus Christ and all that it means, we are on firmer ground than a mere 'Just supposing'. Millions of people ahead of us have weighed it up and come to the breathtaking conclusion that something happened on that first Easter Day that changed our whole view of life. That realization has brought into being the greatest family on earth.

THE GREATEST QUESTION

Death is a subject carefully avoided in conversation today. In a US hospital it was referred to as 'negative patient output'!

Over the centuries we have struggled to buffer ourselves from the ugly spectre of death. We have tried to stem the incoming tide of decay and frailty with every imaginable barricade — money, health programmes, elixirs and ideologies. But at the end of the day the beach has been flattened as though nothing had ever been there.

'If a man dies, shall he live again?' The words from the Bible's book of Job pinpoint our dilemma. More than any other, it has perplexed men and women from the beginning of time.

Stone-age people, tribal people, digital people ... we have all been tantalized by this universal question. Could a warrior take his weapons into a future existence? Should his wife be killed so that she could accompany him in the shadowy spirit-land? Should his slaves, too, be murdered so that his every need could be taken care of?

Whether it was the Nordic Valhalla, the Elysian fields of the Greek philosophers or the carefully mummified processing of Egyptian funeral rites, there was at least some sort of belief in an after-death 'existence'. But it was too vague and shadowy to call it a *life* after death. It was only a transcript of life. It was like a black and white negative after the colourful reality of earthly living.

The world into which Christianity burst for the first time was not short of brilliant thinkers; Greek, Roman and Asian. They all wondered what lay beyond this life. A Homeric region of shades? A Pythagorean series of transmigrations of the soul? An endless cycle of life and death? Nobody actually knew! 'Guesswork is over all,' said Xenophanes.

Then came the message of the resurrection of Jesus. If it had been simply a whispered legend of some unknown person living in Palestine, it might have remained an interesting after-dinner topic of conversation . . . for a while. But here was far more than a story in an ancient book. People were completely transformed in outlook. The personality of Christ blazed out in their conviction. And they were ready to die for their unshakeable confidence in the message of Christ crucified and now alive for ever.

'If a man dies, shall he live again?' A man *had* died. He had died in the full public view of a capital city. He had been crucified as a common criminal. And there were witnesses to his execution. Yet now he *had* come back from the grave. And those who

The early disciples chose to face death rather than worship the old Roman gods.

watched these new believers saw a peace of mind and a freedom of spirit never seen before. They were steadily won over.

The ripples are still spreading today.

AND NOW FOR
THE REST OF THE NEWS . . .

From time to time a report gets out that someone has 'died' — perhaps for an hour or so — and has then returned to life. The stories carry a passing interest. But how long does the excitement last?

There was a case a few years ago like this. A man had 'died' and then came back to life. But the item barely squeezed into the tail end of the news programs. It hardly reached the papers. What was the man's name? Within five minutes no one could remember it. Presumably it will be on a gravestone one day.

In the first century there were no media at all. There was no TV. There were no mass-circulation newspapers or national radio stations. An event needed to be of cyclonic proportions to raise more than a flicker of interest. If Jesus Christ had not, clearly and without doubt, been raised bodily from the grave we would never have heard of him. When sentence had been passed his friends had run away. The demoralized movement would have fizzled out on the launching pad.

Why didn't it fizzle out? Why is it that, Sunday after Sunday, Christian people meet not to mourn Christ's death but to celebrate it? Was there any other death in history that was *celebrated* by the friends of the one who had died? What happened after Jesus' death placed him not in an

*With none of today's technology, the Christian message
spread quickly from person to person.*

obscure footnote to history but at its centre. It is
the pivotal news item that splits the dispensations,
BC from AD.

Is there really any truth in the story?

Chuck Colson was an associate of former US president Richard Nixon. He was involved with Nixon in the Watergate scandal of the seventies, and along with other conspirators he was sent to prison. After serving his prison sentence he spoke of his new-found Christian faith and the forty years in which Christ's disciples never backed down on their witness to the resurrection.

Colson knew from Watergate that truth has a way of slipping out. 'We couldn't hold our stories together for three weeks under that pressure,' he said. 'I was around the most powerful men in the world, but we couldn't hold the lie.'

So the story of the resurrection is remarkable. 'If the resurrection wasn't true,' Colson continued, 'those disciples could never have held out. Someone would have dug out the tape or something!'

A CONFUSING DAY

We should be grateful that we have four accounts, four 'Gospels' to inform us, each from its own standpoint, of the events that took place on the first Easter day.

Jesus had died, executed on a Roman cross, two days before. He had been taken down from

The oldest fragment of a New Testament book is this Greek Gospel of John dating from around AD125.

the cross on the day that was to be called Good Friday. For his followers, it was the darkest day of their lives. Joseph of Arimathea and Nicodemus had placed Jesus' body in a tomb. But in the haste of that evening, with the Jewish day of rest, the sabbath, about to begin, there was a limit to how much could be done.

So the women made their own plans. They intended to get up early, once the sabbath was over, to complete those last funeral rites — a last small service for their friend. That was the plan.

Within minutes the whole thing was scrapped. Forget those spices. Forget the careful binding of the body with linen strips. You thought you were at the tail end of the fiim. You're not — the show is just beginning! You arrived as undertakers, but now you've got a new role. You're the news announcers!

That Sunday morning had ushered in what C.S. Lewis once called 'a new chapter in cosmic history.'

RUNNING FEET

It was a day of disruption for them all. Critics of the Christian faith will sometimes try to set one Gospel report against another. They say that the differences between the accounts discredit the whole event. But what are they asking for? Presumably they would like all four Gospels to be word-for-word identical! And then, of course, their similarity would be used as proof that the whole story was fabricated; that it had been made up and learnt by heart!

It is an added advantage for us to possess these four accounts. If we put them together, we get a single complete picture of confusion and breathless excitement, of people running everywhere. Sometimes one group in its haste just misses another. The day is a turmoil of coming and going.

Half an hour with a pencil and paper, half an hour acting as a detective, will join the four stories into one. And what will surprise you is their restraint. As one writer has put it, 'The most striking feature of the narratives is their homeliness.'

Here is no attempt at a carefully-constructed scenario, with Pontius Pilate or the Jewish high priest falling back in confusion as the resurrected Christ bursts from the tomb in front of thousands of people. The whole thing spills out as a wonderful

More wonderful even than plants coming to life in barren places, the resurrection of Jesus shows how new life can follow death.

jumble, ushering in a new world that will never be the same again.

When the Sabbath was over, Mary Magdalene, Mary the mother of Jesus, and Salome bought spices so that they might go to anoint Jesus' body. Very early on the first day of the week, just after sunrise, they were on their way to the tomb and they asked each other, 'Who will roll the stone away from the entrance of the tomb?'

But when they looked up, they saw the stone, which was very large, had been rolled away. As they entered the tomb, they saw a young man dressed in a white robe sitting on the right side, and they were alarmed.

'Don't be alarmed,' he said. 'You are looking for Jesus the Nazarene, who was crucified. He has risen! He is not here. See the place where they laid him. But go, tell his disciples and Peter, "He is going ahead of you into Galilee. There you will see him, just as he told you."'

Trembling and bewildered, the women went out and fled from the tomb. They said nothing to anyone, because they were afraid.

Mark 16:1-8

I REFUSE TO ANSWER

'If I was able to bring the bones of Jesus Christ before you into this studio, what would it do to your faith?'

This is what Archbishop Michael Ramsay was once asked in an interview. And he gave a memorable reply. 'What you are suggesting is a complete impossibility. It cannot happen, and for that reason I refuse to answer the question.'

'Ah, but I only said *if*,' challenged the interviewer. 'It's simply a hypothesis. *If* I could bring the bones of Christ here, what would it do to your faith?'

Dr. Ramsay remained unmoved. 'I refuse to answer the question.'

But now supposing we look at the issue a little differently. An aspiring author comes up to us, determined to demolish the Christian faith for good. 'I intend to visit the Middle East in order to find, if I can, the bones of Jesus Christ. I want to put an end to all this talk of a resurrection.'

It has happened before. Lew Wallace was resolved to expose what he felt to be the myths of Christianity. So he set out to write a book that would prove once and for all that Jesus never rose from the dead. But his researches led him in an unexpected direction, and he began to find himself believing. He confided to his wife that he would now be unable to write the book. 'Write another one then,' she urged.

Ben Hur, with its compelling story of Christ, was the result. Later it became a film that inspired audiences all over the world.

It happened too with Frank Morison. His attempt to uncover the 'real' unembroidered story of Jesus turned into what he later described as 'the book that refused to be written'. It became instead the best-seller *Who Moved the Stone?* On page after page, Morison shows how the most reasonable conclusion is that Jesus did rise from death.

The Christian faith can stand up to the most rigorous of investigations. But can we really *prove* the evidence? Or, even then, would we have other psychological or moral barriers?

The Gospel records provide clear evidence that Jesus rose from the dead.

A QUESTION OF EVIDENCE

Of course we can never *prove* the resurrection of
Jesus, with mathematical, logical proof. But, like
any other event which claims to be historically true,
we can piece together the evidence and draw our
own conclusion.

We may accept as fact that Tensing and Hilary
were the first to climb Everest. The world believed
their claim on the strength of their words and a
photograph.

So what are the pointers to the truth of the
bodily resurrection of Jesus?

The empty tomb. All agree that it was empty.
But there are only three explanations to account
for this fact:

● *Jesus' friends took his body.* All the evidence
indicates that the events of Good Friday broke
the spirit of the disciples completely. The idea
of a resurrection, contrived or real, seems to have
been very far from their thoughts. And in any case
a guard was set over the tomb. So this explanation
does not fit the facts.

● *His enemies removed the body.* What would be the
motive? Such an act could only have promoted the
very thing they feared — rumors that Jesus was

alive. Instead they took precautions and set a guard.

● *Jesus rose again from death.* The only explanation that fits the data is that Jesus was raised from death on the third day.

The resurrection appearances. Following his resurrection Jesus appeared to his followers. Some ten different instances are described to us. Some involve one or two witnesses, some more. On occasions all eleven disciples were present, and once there were 500 people.

These are no hallucinations. The appearances took place at different times of day, out of doors and indoors, and to whole groups of people. The appearances were not limited to isolated individuals with particular psychological needs.

And then, at a certain point, the appearances stopped abruptly. Those who are subject to dreams, visions or hallucinations tend to go on having them.

The changed disciples. Not even the smallest dent would have been made upon the world unless the disciples had been changed. But they were new people! They became fired with confidence and joy at the amazing things that had happened.

The world of Judaism, the world of Greek thought, Roman imperialism — they would have known nothing about Jesus Christ had it not been for the transformed disciples. It was his followers who were to carry the message — the same men who had fled in fear when Jesus was first arrested. Before long they would be facing lions . . .

Christianity was to outgrow both Judaism and Greek culture. One day the Church would stand at the grave of the Caesars. It would undergird future civilizations. It would replace the traditional Jewish sabbath with the Christian day associated with the resurrection. Only people who knew for sure that an epoch-making event had occurred would have gone to the extent of interfering with such a centuries-old custom.

After rising from the dead Jesus appeared to his disciples by Lake Galilee.

Is there some discrepancy between Jesus' clear prediction that he would rise again after three days and three nights of burial, and the actual event? If he was crucified on the Friday and raised on the Sunday morning, then in fact he was only in the tomb for two nights.

It's as well to sort this out, in view of the fact that critics of the Christian faith will point to this issue and try to make capital out of it. What perhaps they do not know is that there was a Jewish principle of reckoning, according to which a part of any period covered by a night and a day counted as the whole period. Thus, a whole day and part of two other days would be counted as three days and three nights.

Let's look at an example. In the Old Testament book of Esther, we learn that the young queen Esther appeals for a fast to be observed on her behalf, in which no one will eat or drink for three days, night or day. Then we read that 'On the third day, Esther put on her royal robes,' the fast being over, as she prepared to face the king. In fact, only two nights had elapsed. Nevertheless, in Jewish thinking three days and three nights would have been ticked off in the chronology.

So it was with entire accuracy — but in a Jewish mode of thinking — that Christ predicted that 'as Jonah was three days and three nights in the belly of the fish, so will the Son of man be three days and three nights in the heart of the earth.'

THE PSYCHOLOGICAL BARRIER

There are those who maintain that Jesus never rose.
They say such was the force of his character that his
influence lived on. The early Christian preachers
meant only this continuing strength of personality
when they talked of the resurrection.

But such theories fly straight in the face of the
sources available to us.

Some writers assert that the teaching of the
bodily resurrection of Jesus has to be regarded as a
myth. But do these writers treat the death of Jesus
in this way? Or his burial? The Bible refers to the
resurrection in the same matter-of-fact way as it
speaks of his death.

An early convert, known to us as St. Paul, wrote
to a church in Corinth, 'For I delivered to you as
of first importance what I also received, that Christ
died for our sins in accordance with the scriptures,
that he was *buried*, that he was *raised* on the third
day in accordance with the scriptures, and that he
appeared . . . '

Would the critics say that the first two events
are historical but that the last two are mythical? On
what basis can we play games like that with a single
sentence? Always there is this mention of 'the third
day.' It sounds like a statement of a factual event.
How could it mean otherwise?

Some critics believe that it is the *meaning*,

the concept of resurrection, that is important in the experience and character of believing people. It doesn't matter if Christ's body is still in the tomb!

But as another writer asks, 'If the early Christians who used the story of the empty tomb understood it simply as myth and nothing more, why should anyone want to oppose their message?'

Such teaching hardly sounds like the material of which martyrs are made, or from which new churches are formed.

If a real resurrection was going to take place, then it would have to be Jesus. He was, after all, the greatest moral giant the human race has ever known. Had we been told that one of the Caesars had been resurrected, or Aristotle, or Alexander the Great, we might have smiled accommodatingly at the tale. But then we would have left it alone.

But the fact that the event centres upon Jesus has made millions think again. Has anyone come even close to him in spiritual stature and moral authority? The Jewish historian Josephus, who was no friend of the Christian faith, wrote, 'Now there was about this time Jesus, a wise man, if it be lawful to call him a man . . . '

His acceptance of the worship of others, his

Crossing from death to life is like crossing a great bridge – between an old life and a new life in Jesus.

forgiveness of people's sins, his claims of equality with God would seem to be a sure route to becoming the most arrogant egoist of all time. But the thinking world — believing and unbelieving, Jewish, Muslim or Hindu — has never said that of Jesus. The evidence is all in the opposite direction. The pages of the Gospels shine with his authority, goodness and compassion.

THE MORAL BARRIER

I once spoke with a student who turned out to be an
atheist. Theology was his subject, and I asked him
why he had chosen it. 'It amuses me,' he said.

Amused? Bored? Eternal truths are unlikely
to have anything to say to those who live on
a superficial level. It doesn't matter how well-
equipped they may be intellectually.

We can know all the arguments. We can even
be convinced in an academic kind of way about the
validity of the Christian claim that Christ is alive.
We can have a flirtation with the faith and listen to
TV sermons. But it all amounts to nothing if there
is something within that says 'Keep away' to the
Lord of the Easter dawn.

The first-century puppet king Agrippa wanted
to keep his distance. He held St. Paul in prison,
yet was intrigued by his beliefs. When tried before
him Paul asked the court, 'Why is it thought
incredible by any of you that God raises the
dead?'

Agrippa heard Paul's explanation, but at the
end turned it into a joke. 'In a short time you
think to make me a Christian!' he quipped. But
the Herods were like that. Agrippa's great-uncle,
Herod Antipas, had hoped for a little light enter-
tainment from his brief encounter with Jesus, but
got bored and sent his silent prisoner back to

Only as we commit ourselves to Christ do we discover the life he offers.

Pontius Pilate.

Again and again, the major barrier that prevents people believing in the resurrection of Jesus Christ is their willingness to be committed, not a matter of evidence at all.

The resurrection is the supreme miracle lying at the heart of the Christian revelation. But it is a very inconvenient truth.

It upsets many of our preconceived ideas. It interferes with our plans. It forces us to reckon with the certainty that one day we shall meet with this central figure of history. The resurrection makes us re-evaluate our goals, priorities and programmes. It gets in our way!

When St Peter first preached that Christ was alive, his listeners were 'cut to the heart'. It was not good news to them. Many of them had been in Jerusalem at the time of the crucifixion. Some of them had been bystanders that fateful day, participants in the terrible events which had led to the murder of the long-expected Messiah, the promised deliverer of Israel.

Now they were heartbroken. The resurrection is not good news to the man or woman who wants to have nothing to do with the risen Jesus. It is preferable to say, 'I don't believe', or even, 'I won't believe'. It is better to hug oneself into hoping that the issue will go away.

Alternatively we may do as those first listeners did in Jerusalem. Cut to the heart they may have been, but the day ended with the membership of the Christian family having ballooned by over 2,000 per cent!

THE DOUBTER

On the evening of that day, the first day
of the week, the doors being shut where
the disciples were, for fear of the Jews,
Jesus came and stood among them and
said to them, 'Peace be with you.' When
he had said this, he showed them his
hands and his side. Then the disciples
were glad when they saw the Lord.

John 20:19-20

There is a world of understatement in the
Gospel's reporting. I can be 'glad' if the train
arrives on time. But this was the undiluted, heart-
felt joy of individuals whose world had folded under
them only forty-eight hours earlier. To have their
leader with them — triumphant over death, talking
with them, eating with them — it was beyond
description. Yes, they were glad.

But where was Thomas?

We now know this disciple as 'Doubting
Thomas'. We have come to associate him with
pessimism. It was in his character to absent himself,
to retreat from a cold hostile world and to wrap
himself in his own misgivings.

When the others told him the overwhelming,
brilliant news of their Sunday evening encounter,

Thomas the missing disciple becomes Thomas the doubting disciple: 'Unless I see in his hands the print of the nails, and place my finger in the mark of the nails, and place my hand in his side, I will not believe.'

That is why we call him the Doubter. And yet in one sense Thomas was a little too *sure* of himself. Was there any real reason to distrust the word of people he had been with for the past three years? Isolated by his absence, and insulated by his temperament, he talks like someone in our Western self-centered world. 'But I can't believe that,' they insist. His outlook is completely determined by the point at which he himself is standing. Here is doubt at its most dogmatic and intolerant: *I will not believe.*

We don't hold Thomas' morose nature against him, any more than we congratulate an outgoing person for being born with a sunny smile. No, we don't blame Thomas for being Thomas. But perhaps we should hold him accountable for not *knowing* that he was Thomas.

'Do you know yourself?' is a good question for a doubter. Do you recognize and take account of your personality, background and prejudices when forming your opinions? At this time of crisis Thomas was more liable to be governed by his emotions than by anything else. Yet what he needed was the ability to *think*. He needed to remember what Christ had earlier taught them all. And he also needed the support of the group. As it was, emotions and isolation took over: *I will not believe.*

A week later his disciples were in the
house again, and Thomas was with
them. Though the doors were locked,
Jesus came and stood among them, and
said, 'Peace be with you!' Then he said
to Thomas, 'Put your finger here, see
my hands. Reach out your hand and
put it into my side. Stop doubting
and believe.'
Thomas answered, 'My Lord and
my God!'
John 20:26-28

Naturally, we are grateful for the sequel to
the story. It gives us Thomas' words of full and
unqualified recognition when he was finally faced
by Jesus: 'My Lord and my God.'

The rejoinder of Jesus to the doubter also
reassures the many who, like Thomas, have wanted
to say, 'If only I could see, meet, touch . . . then
I would believe.' The reports of the original
first-hand witnesses are enough for faith. 'Happy
are those who have not seen and yet believe,'
Jesus said.

*It's up to the individual to decide how he or she will respond
to the fact of the empty tomb.*

Is it true to say of Christ's resurrection that it had never happened before? What about Jesus' raising of the young man from Nain, of Jairus' daughter, or — supremely — Lazarus after four days in the tomb? (If you want to check out the references to these stories, see the back of this book.)

We cannot in fact accurately describe these biblical events as *resurrections* — at least not in the same terms as apply to Christ's raising. Take for instance the story of Lazarus. Here is one of the great 'signs' of Christ's divine identity. His authority is stamped all over the passage as he demonstrates his power over death. 'Take the stone away! . . . Lazarus, come out! . . . Untie him and let him go!'

Let him go? Go where? Why, back to the house in Bethany which Lazarus shared with his sisters Martha and Mary. It would be lunch-time in a few minutes. Maybe it was the turn of Lazarus to do the washing today — you don't mind, do you, Lazarus? Oh, and the tax returns have got to be filled in right away — you hadn't forgotten, had you?

That was the difference. The raising of Lazarus was a marvelous thing, but Lazarus had been brought *back again* — into this old decaying world, with its struggles and chores, its aches, pains and heartaches — and one day he would go through the whole process of dying all over again.

So the raising of Lazarus by no means supplies us with our definition of 'resurrection'. His raising was more like the previews shown before a movie; it was like the curtain-raiser. The big event was to be the resurrection of Jesus from death — never to die again. Lazarus' return from the grave was a *resuscitation*; it was a coming *back*. Christ's resurrection was a going *on*, with a new body, to a life that had utterly transcended death.

THE RESURRECTION BODY

> But some will ask, 'How are the dead
> raised? With what kind of body do
> they come?'
>
> *1 Corinthians 15:35*

It is a natural question for followers of Jesus to pose. After all, he is the forerunner of us all. He was raised, and we are to be raised, with bodies like his, one day. It is a staggering concept. Think of those resurrection appearances. Here was no shadowy ghost: for ghosts don't eat grilled fish.

'Touch me, and see,' he said, 'for a spirit has not flesh and bones as you see that I have.' And yet this body could pass through closed doors. Here is a new dimension of existence altogether. *It will be ours one day*. So naturally questions arise about the resurrection body.

● **How can we be sure that there is such a thing?** Because of Christ's own resurrection. The resurrection life resides in him. 'I am the resurrection and the life,' he told Martha; 'he who believes in me, though he die, yet shall he live, and whoever lives and believes in me shall never die.' It is a promise, a promise no less wonderful than another that is repeated four times in all, that Christ will raise up all who are his at the last day.

Can that dimension of existence be any less real, less substantial, less fulfilling than the one we experience now? It will be life enhanced beyond our present comprehension. The best, by far the best, is yet to come!

● **How similar will the resurrection body be to our earthly body?** It will be related to our earthly bodies — with a real continuity — but with a major difference. It will be a perfect and glorious body, like that of Jesus. There will be no process of decay, no ageing.

It will also be what St Paul called 'a spiritual body'. To us that sounds like a contradiction in terms. But when the new order begins, the bodies that Christ's followers will be given will be as suitable to the new environment as tropical clothes would be for life on the equator.

● **What will the resurrection body be like?** It will be 'like his glorious body'. If so, it will be recognizable (as Christ's was), with unusual powers.

A caution, however; for Jesus' body, though 'spiritual', was still capable of being here on earth. It is conceivable that there could be a difference

The resurrection life is a whole new order of existence, just as the life of a butterfly is totally different from that of the chrysalis.

between the body that the disciples saw after the resurrection and Christ's glorified body in heaven. If there is any difference, we are not told about it.

● When will we receive this body? It will happen in a moment, 'in the twinkling of an eye, at the last trumpet,' when 'we shall be changed.' Until that point, believers who have died are described as being 'asleep': asleep, that is, from the point of view of those who remain alive; as far as the dead are concerned they are 'away from the body and at home with the Lord,' awaiting Christ's second coming when they will rise and be given new bodies.

● Why doesn't the Bible tell us more about it? Because it concentrates on the most important feature of all regarding the future. Jesus said that 'where I am you may be also' . . . 'So we shall always be with the Lord.'

It is Christ's glorified and kingly presence that will dominate in the next life. It will be wonderful because *he* is there. The Bible does not go into any great detail on the secondary issues. What matters is the wonderful prospect highlighted in the language of the traditional King James version of the Bible:

> 'Eye hath not seen, nor ear heard,
> neither have entered into the heart
> of man, the things which God hath
> prepared for them that love him.'

A WAY OF LIFE

The resurrection is more than a distant hope. The resurrection life begins the moment that Christ is accepted by faith as Lord and Savior. Christians are 'raised with Christ'. *They have already been raised.* The new life with him is already a present reality.

● **We live at a different altitude**. We are to 'seek the things that are above, where Christ is'. We may be living in a back street with high rises on every side. But our life with Jesus Christ, strengthened by a daily prayer fellowship with him, enables us to live with and rise above the pressures that crowd in on us from every side.

● **We see from a different perspective**. 'Set your minds on things that are above,' declares the apostle Paul, 'not on things that are on the earth.' 'Aim at heaven,' said C.S. Lewis, 'and you will get earth thrown in as well; aim at earth, and you will get neither.' It is the resurrection dimension that gives purpose and direction to life on earth.

● **We grow in a different environment**. Again, to quote Paul, 'For you have died, and your life is hid with Christ in God.' Part One of the Christian's life is a closed book. It's 'dead.'

The new order has begun in identification with Jesus Christ. He was dead, and we 'died' with him. But he is alive for ever, and we can know his 'eternal' life. Our life is hid with him. Our destinies are bound up with him. It is the world of the kingdom of God, and it will last for ever.

● **We look at a different horizon**. For, Paul says, 'When Christ who is our life appears, then you also will appear with him in glory.' The follower of Jesus is a child of eternity, a citizen of heaven.

For the children of the resurrection, we are not traveling towards decay and disintegration, nor towards the darkness of approaching night. The book of Proverbs speaks vividly of the coming dawn:

'The road the righteous travel is like the sunrise, getting brighter and brighter, until daylight has come.'

The resurrection of Jesus gives us a hope for the future that nothing can take from us: he rose again – it's a real historical fact. We too will rise to new life if we put our trust in him.

It was Easter Sunday morning. Ugandan pastor Kefa Sempangi returned to his house after taking the morning service — to run into an ambush from a gang of five killers.

'We are going to kill you,' said the leader. 'If you have anything to say, say it before you die.'

Kefa began to shake. They won't need to kill me, he thought. I am going to fall over dead. But then, as he recalls, 'From far away I heard a voice, and I was astonished to realize that it was my own. "I do not need to plead my own cause," I heard myself saying. "I am a dead man already. My life is dead and hidden in Christ. It is your lives that are in danger, you are dead in your sins. I will pray to God that after you have killed me, he will spare you from eternal destruction."'

The leader stepped forward; his face had changed. 'Will you pray for us now?' he asked. It was the turning-point. All five men were to become members of Kefa's church.

CHECK THE FACTS!

If you would like to look up some of the evidence for yourself, it is found in the following Bible passages. The references are to the Bible book, then the chapter, then the verse number.

Page 16	Matthew 28:1-10,16-20; Mark 16
Page 26	Matthew 12:40
Page 27	1 Corinthians 15:4
Page 33	Acts 26
Pages 34-36	John 20-21
Page 38	Luke 7:11-17 Matthew 9:18-26; Mark 5:21-43; Luke 8:40-56 John 11: 1-44
Page 39	Luke 24, John 6:39ff; 11:25-26
Page 40	1 Corinthians 15:35ff; Philippians 3:21
Page 42	2 Corinthians 5:8; 1 Corinthians 2:9
Page 43	Colossians 3:1-3
Page 46	1 Thessalonians 4:16-17; Colossians 3:4; Proverbs 4:18